FATHERED WHILE FATHERLESS

A SON FINDING HIS WAY

MICHEAL WELLINGTON

KP PUBLISHING COMPANY

Copyright 2019 by Micheal Wellington
All rights reserved. In accordance with the U.S. Copyright Act of 1976, the scanning, uploading, and electronic sharing of any part of this book without the permission of the publisher is unlawful piracy and theft of the author's intellectual property. If you would like to use material from this book (other than for review purposes), prior written permission must be obtained by contacting the publisher at info@knowledgepowerinc.com

Thank you for your support of the author's rights.

ISBN: 978-1-950936-15-1 (Paperback)
ISBN: 978-1-950936-16-8 (E-book)
Library of Congress Control Number: 2019909263

Editors: Steve Robinson and Stacie Fujii
Cover Design: Juan Roberts, Creative Lunacy, Inc.
Interior Design: Jennifer Houle
Literary Director: Sandra L. Slayton

Unless otherwise indicated, Scripture quotations are from the Holy Bible, New International Version®. NIV®. Copyright© 1973, 1978, 1984, 2011 by Biblica, Inc.™ Used by permission of NavPress. All rights reserved. Represented by Tyndale House Publishers, Inc.

Published by:
KP Publishing Company
Publisher of Fiction, Nonfiction & Children's Books
Valencia, CA 91355

Printed in the United States of America

DEDICATION

This book is dedicated first, to my Heavenly Father who placed many obstacles in my way to get me to bump my head, make bad decisions, persevere, and conquer those things, to create the man that I am today.

To my wife, Tina, who has dealt with me, loved me, stood by me, encouraged me, and pushed me the entire time I had highs and lows on this journey. I love you more each day.

To my mother, I have realized as I've grown that you did everything you could to raise me. You did the best with what you had. I am sorry that I 've hurt you or made you cry.

To my daughter, Grace, I hope that once you grow old, you'll know that I've loved you since your conception. I want to be the best representation of Christ, and a father that I can be for you.

To Mr. Jackson, who God used to help me forgive. You taught me to find love in a father, who was not my father. You helped me tear down the wall of hate that was built up for 30 plus years. I am forever grateful.

Finally, to my biological father, whoever you are, I dedicate this book to you because I understand that things happen in life, but I want you to know that I have forgiven you. Hopefully one day we will meet.

With all sincerity,
Micheal Wellington

FOREWORD

The scars in a man's heart are often profound. The deepest emotional wound many will ever experience will be inflicted by their father. This was no different for Micheal. Through abuse, neglect, and/or abandonment, a father-wound often distorts one's self-perception, and leads to the inability to be authentic.

As a clinician, coach, and minister, I often say, "Vulnerability and authenticity are two sides of the wellness coin." Yung Pueblo says, "taking a moment to figure out how you really feel—instead of letting patterns decide for you—is one of the most authentic things you can do." This process requires courageous authenticity, deep self-awareness, and vulnerable self-reflection.

Courageous vulnerability is the first step for developing compassion, empathy, and cultivating healthy relationships—including the healthy relationship with self. It takes courage to address the narratives we tell ourselves about who we are. Prolonged exposure to repetitive or severe events such as child abuse, neglect, and abandonment can negatively skew the narrative we construct for ourselves.

Before I help individuals identify who they are, I help them to identify whose they are. Therefore, the starting point in the healing journey begins with one's relationship with GOD. Of all the ways God could have chosen to relate to humanity, He chose the language of family. God declares that He is our Heavenly Father. The role of a father is key to our humanity and journey to wholeness.

Often the scars of life leave deep impressions upon our souls. These wounds can prevent us from embracing our true identity as a child of God. His intention from the beginning was always for us to know our identity in Him.

When we acknowledge God, submit to His will, His Word and promises, we can find freedom in our relationships, in our walk of faith, and in our calling to be all He created us to be.

Proverbs 23:7 states that as a man thinks in his heart, so is he. Our thoughts have a profound effect on our emotional condition. We may not realize how our thoughts affect our feelings and perception of reality. Most of us assume it is the other way around; that our feelings and reality come first— and our thoughts naturally follow. But as we watch the relationship between thoughts and feelings, we begin to recognize that our mindset and thoughts inform our feelings and reality.

Micheal's journey to healing required identifying that he had a father-wound. Now after courageous work, Mike's life is best described by the term KAIZEN or continuous improvement (KAI means change, and ZEN means better). Mike embraced this courageous kaizen journey by exploring his thoughts, feelings, and behaviors. It became clear to Mike that his father-wound influenced and reinforced an incorrect and toxic perception of himself. As Micheal continued in his healing journey, he also wanted more from the Lord and the answer to this longing was greater intimacy with his Heavenly Father. True intimacy is often developed in solitude with God. Intimacy (In-to-me-you-see) is shared and experienced in a safe place often apart from others. As we seek and experience a deeper relationship with God, our Heavenly Father helps us to reject the toxic labels we had attached to ourselves. Once released from these untruths, a cleansing wholeness can take place.

Micheal was able to declare God's Word over his life. He embraced Jeremiah 17:14, "Heal me, O LORD, and I will be healed; save me and I will be saved, for you are the One I praise." Micheal claimed Jeremiah 30:17, "But I, God, will restore you to health and heal your wounds, declares the LORD."

It has been a true honor to be a part of Mike's life narrative and see the amazing growth in his intimacy with God. I have watched with great joy as Mike has stepped into his role as a wonderful husband and dad. My biggest privilege is being the godfather to Mike's beautiful daughter, Grace.

In this book, you will have the honor of journeying with Mike as he vulnerably and courageously shares his story of abandonment and a lack of attachment to a male figure. You will have the pleasure of seeing what the journey of wholeness and healing can look like when we embrace who we are and Whose we are!

Jason Plunkett
PsyD in Psychology (Organizational Leadership emphasis)
USA Director for ZOE International (Combating Human Sex Trafficking)

CONTENTS

Dedication v

Foreword vii

CHAPTER 1: *I Affirm You with, "You are Ugly, You are Dark"* 1

CHAPTER 2: *A Father? What's That* 13

CHAPTER 3: *My Mother Will Do, But . . .* 19

CHAPTER 4: *I Longed for a Relationship* 27

CHAPTER 5: *Me, Kids? Never!* 41

CHAPTER 6: *If You Love Me, Then Why?* 51

CHAPTER 7: *You Are Not The Father* 65

CHAPTER 8: *Surrender It All to Me* 77

CHAPTER 9: *Let Me Love You* 87

CHAPTER 10: *Does God Really Forgive?* 99

About the Author 103

Acknowledgment 107

CHAPTER 1
I AFFIRM YOU WITH "YOU ARE UGLY, YOU ARE DARK!"

Every single organism that is on earth is created with a seed. From that seed, the organism will surely grow. Every mammal, reptile, plant, and tree must be planted deep into an egg or soil. From there, the organism grows, and life begins. Affirmation is also a seed. The words that are spoken to a child at a young age are implanted for life. The Bible says that there is life and death in the power of the tongue. You can create the most confident, or the most insecure child with just a couple of words.

Affirmation should be started early in a child's life, because what you speak to that child will resonate within them for the rest of their lives. Therefore, speak life. If you don't speak life what you are saying can destroy them.

We have all heard the phrase "Sticks and stones may break my bones, but words will never hurt me." This is false. Being brutally beaten, scarred, having bones broken, and even being shot, are all situations where your body heals itself. I think God made us all X-men.

Words, on the other hand, hurt more than all those things. Words can cause fear. Words can totally scar us. Words can make us ugly in spite of the greatness, vastness, and beauty that God created in us.

Even as a history teacher, I am still not all the way certain that the Willie Lynch letter was written, but the principles are true and are very present. The Willie Lynch letter was written in the 1700's for slave master's to give them a specific plan to make sure their slaves never revolted against them. The main premise was, "You keep a slave in bondage by mentally oppressing them, turning them against one another, and making them hate themselves because of their appearance." This letter, though written centuries ago, had an everlasting impact on our African American people. This was definitely the case with me. Coloration was always in my face. Webster's dictionary defines ugly as offensive to the sight; hideous." It also defines dark as not fair in complexion.

Micheal (Age 7)

In my childhood I heard these two words paired together as casually as the words; peanut butter and jelly, shoes and socks and soap and water. Growing up, I hated being dark skinned. I was made to feel like it was the worst thing you could do to a child, allowing them to grow up being dark skinned.

One of my sisters, who is closest to me in age, was dark like me. My mother, brother, and youngest sister's complexions were a lighter skin tone. For the most part, my sister and I had similar negative feelings regarding our being darker than the rest of our family members.

One thing I wished I would've known as a kid, that I know now, is that I had the mind to affirm my siblings, even though I was just a tad older than them. Our outcomes on how we saw ourselves may have been different as we grew into adolescence and adult years. When I was younger, I wanted to be white or light skinned. Why? Because, as a result of hearing things like "you black mutha _____," and "you are ugly because you are dark," I assumed that not being as dark as I was, must've been a lot easier to manage.

I sang in a choir as a young kid. Every February during Black History we would sing this song titled "Black is So Beautiful." "Black is so beautiful. Black is so beautiful. Black is so beautiful, and it's so beautiful, beautiful to be black." I had to lead the song. Though everyone around would talk about how cute the song was, I never believed the words of it. Black was not beautiful to me. They were just words to a song. You can't expect me to believe this song, just to go back into this world and hear the exact opposite.

I AFFIRM YOU WITH "YOU ARE UGLY, YOU ARE DARK!"

Going into junior high, because of my broken self-image, I was solely attracted to girls who were either lighter skinned, mixed, or not black at all. I tended to believe that if I ever had a kid, I would not want my child to be dark skinned because, like I was told, being dark was ugly. I would not want another child to have my experience. I also knew that if the kid were created with a mixed, or non-black female, the child would be beautiful. That is what we are taught through observation, as well as through the media. This was my mindset for a long time.

Growing up the only women I ever saw being uplifted as beautiful were the light, fairer skinned women. I saw them with my uncles. I saw them on television. I saw them everywhere. Everyone had to have a light-skinned woman with long hair.

High school was probably the worst part of the ugly and dark experience. I liked so many light-skinned girls, and they would just diss me hard. "No, I am sorry. You are too dark," one girl said. "I only date light-skin guys with green eyes," another girl said. "You are ugly," another girl said.

They had no filters. I heard this for my first two years of high school. There was one girl who was a freshman also and she was mixed, light-skinned, and had long hair. We had a class together and she would talk to me.

I was intimidated, but excited that someone lighter than me would be attracted to someone as ugly as me. At this point in my life, an almost fifteen-year-old boy, I was still a virgin. In my quest to feel wanted and attractive to the opposite sex, especially someone lighter than me, the opportunity came a month and four days before my fifteenth birthday.

Even as this was about to take place, I still felt ugly. I had no idea what was about to happen. We caught the bus to one of my childhood friend's house. We were talking for a while and then we began kissing each other. At this point I was literally shaking with fear. She says, "Isn't this what you want," as she begins to undress me. In the back of my mind I am thinking this is about to happen, but I also did not want the consequences that could also follow.

After we concluded, I started to tear up for a couple of reasons. I couldn't believe I had just lost my virginity in the length of a couple of minutes. Secondly, I thought, what if she becomes pregnant. I was too young to have a child. She quickly eased part of the worry by stating that she was on birth control. From that day forward, I vowed that I would never engage in sex until I was married.

Where was pops to teach me about this stuff?

Going into eleventh grade, I moved with my aunt, Charmaine, in Canyon Country, California. I went to live with my aunt for several reasons. Academically, I didn't agree with school. My aunt changed that quickly. She made it known that education was important in her home, and if I did not adhere, I was going back home. I did not want to go back home. Canyon Country was different, and nothing like what I was used to. I also believe it was divine intervention that I went to live in Canyon Country. My aunt, and late uncle Manuel, were the only real examples of a family with a husband-wife I had seen. They were the examples of how parents were toward their children regarding discipline, love, and everything in between.

The demographics in Canyon Country were much different than Pacoima. The majority were white, and the Latino community was also fairly large. In this area, there were hardly any black people. If I am not mistaken, there was a grand total of twelve black kids at the high school. All of the black girls were mixed. I thought I would have a better chance with these girls, due to the lack of black males. I was wrong. There were two girls that I was very attracted to. Both had the same reaction to me.

"I don't like dark guys."

Until this day, I am not sure how true it is, but according to their closest friends, they mentioned to them that I was ugly. Go figure. Because of this, I started to only flirt with women who were not black. It seemed that the white girls liked me, so I was going to entertain that. Plus, it still fell in line with my thinking of, "my future children will be beautiful if I have a child with a non-black woman." I kept my vow of no sex until marriage, but other things did happen in this period of my life.

The first time I heard a woman tell me I was beautiful; I didn't believe it. I was seventeen years old, and she was a little older than me. She was kind of like my cousin because I had known her pretty much my entire life. Her name was

Doris. She was the oldest of three sisters. I did not believe her, because no one had ever told me that. Plus, women, not men, are beautiful. At least that is what I thought.

"You are a beautiful young chocolate man. Out of all of the bunch, you will be the most attractive as you get older." In the midst of me blushing, because of her words, in the back of my mind, I absolutely did not believe a word she said. The wound of being the ugly dark kid had already been established, and it would take a lot of work to heal.

Teenage boys have a joking way of projecting how we feel onto other people so that we feel better about ourselves. In high school we would all tell each other how ugly the other person was, and everyone would laugh. I was typically the loudest when these sessions would take place. The point was to hit first so that you weren't hit. I hated being called ugly. I would laugh, because that's what you were supposed to do. Inwardly, it would reopen "ugly" wounds.

"Dirty black kid" was another name I would be called. Truth be told, I was a dirty black kid. If you have ever seen kid pictures from the 60s in the South, sitting on the porch with peddle pusher pants, no shoes, and ashy, that was me. Because of that, as I got older and entered college, I would always try to look fly. I would put on my best outfits so that people wouldn't mistake me for being dirty, black, or ugly.

This negative outlook that I had about myself carried over into every part of my life. I was pessimistic about everything. "We can't do this," or "that is impossible," and "we shouldn't even bother," were my favorite things to say. I believe I missed out on a lot because every deep-rooted wound I had would further cause me to not believe in my possibilities.

The most difficult part of having the deep wounds of being ugly and dark was when I met my wife, Tina. I will explain about Tina a little later. This was the second time I was told that I was beautiful, but it was on a consistent basis. While we were dating, she would constantly tell me how attractive I was, but I never accepted it. I would always deflect her words, because again, to me, it's not true. "Stop lying," would be my consistent response. I could not accept the fact that someone thought so highly of me, since no one did while growing up. My wall had already been built, and it was sturdy enough to never allow anyone to tear it down. It took years of her praying to God that eventually opened my eyes to see what she had been telling me for so long. I am beautiful. I am loved. I am special. I am fearfully and wonderfully made.

You are too! Always remember, use your words wisely.

Speak Life!

CHAPTER 2
A FATHER? WHAT'S THAT?

Webster's dictionary defines a father as a male who begets a child. He is PRESENT for his children, NOURISHES and NURTURES them.

The Bible has many phrases about the Father. Our Heavenly Father will NEVER leave or FORSAKE us. There is NOTHING that will SEPARATE us from the Father's love. The Father LOVED the world so much that he sacrificed his own son, so that we could have eternal life.

I had never felt, nor seen this version of a father in my life ever . . . but, it was something that I desired to have, all my life. I believe things may have been different with me as a young boy if I had a present and nurturing father present.

Father's Day happens on the second weekend in June, every year. It is a day where individuals with father's take time out to acknowledge them for being great men. It was a day that made kids like me, who didn't have a father, envy those who did, (though there were very few where I was from).

Father's Day was a day that I absolutely hated for a large portion of my life. In high school I started to call this day "Deadbeat Awareness Day," because it was the day that I truly realized I did not have a father. Of all my close friends and acquaintances, one of them had a father that exhibited all the characteristics mentioned above. This was another reasons I did not want to have a child. Though I tried hard to fight the fact that I was insecure, I had no clue on how to be a father because I had no real models and did not want to fail.

So, when people would say "Happy Father's Day" to me before I had a child I would always respond "I am not a father." Their response would always be the same. "You father a lot of the kids that you work with on a daily basis." They were right, but I chose not to see it that way.

I met someone who became a close friend; almost a brother. At the time, he was only known as Jason Plunkett. A guy that my wife had known since she was four years old. Their parents knew each other from the country of Belize. I had known of Jason since 2000 but did not really "know" him until we ended up at the same church. After a few months of having this new-found relationship with him, my heart started to dramatically soften. I started seeing situations more emphatically. Even my wife said that I seemed like a "sweeter" person. I am not sure if that was a good or bad thing, but I was different. My speech on wanting children had now become, "I'm not sure, but if God wants me to have children, then I will submit my will to His." Though this was my mindset, in the subconscious, I still hesitated, I still had "daddy issues" of my own.

It took me almost thirty-four years to acknowledge that I did indeed have daddy problems. I attempted to suppress these feelings and say things like "no I don't have daddy problems." My wife constantly wanted me to find my father. "Why do you want me to find him? I don't want to find him. He left me," I would say.

On one such day the Lord was dealing with me hard; extremely hard. I had an episode where my encounter was so strong that I began to cry. One Sunday at church, I had a vision that the Holy Spirit was hugging me. As He squeezed, I squeezed myself just as hard. Suddenly it felt as if the Holy Spirit was slowly walking away from me. I began to plead, "please don't leave."

I was getting hugged, loved, and affirmed all in the same setting. That was probably the greatest encounter that I have ever had, because it was an experience that I wanted with an earthly father. *"Just hold me, tell me that you are proud of me, that I am doing good things in your eyes."* That's all I wanted. These were things that I did not hear growing up as a young adolescent boy, and I so desperately wanted them.

As everything in the service got back to "normal" I opened my eyes only to find that I was the only person in the entire church still standing up. I was so into my own zone that I didn't care. When you have an encounter with the God of the Universe, who takes time out to personally visit you, you must take full advantage. You never know when that glorious moment will take place again.

I can laugh about it now, but it was kind of embarrassing at the time. As time passed and the alter call began, I was looking around the church. My eyes were red, my body was weak, and I was still high on the God encounter I had an hour earlier.

As I scanned the room no-one caught my eye. Suddenly I spotted one of my friends in the center aisle, two rows behind me. It was not that I just spotted him, but the position he was in gave me an epiphany that I had daddy issues. He was holding his daughter in his arms while holding his son's hand as he attentively listened to what the pastor was speaking on.

I went home that day to reveal to my wife that I did suffer from deep rooted pain and anger. But despite all that, God had changed something inside of me. I felt different. I knew it was a combination of my friends praying for me, my budding relationship with my friend, Jason Plunkett, and God's intervention that evening. After that day, I no longer called Father's Day deadbeat awareness day. I started saying, "Happy Father's Day," to men who I knew had children.

I believed the preparation for my own future Father's Day was in the making.

CHAPTER 3
MY MOTHER WILL DO, BUT...

My entire adolescent life, all I wanted to do was to be loved. I wanted a happy-go-lucky family like I saw on the white television shows I watched as a kid. They all had the entire family with the mother and father. They would have the family gatherings. The father would have deep conversations with the kids about life and the opposite sex. He would teach them how to catch a ball. These were all the things I was thirsting for. I just wanted to be affirmed.

Unfortunately, I never was.

My mother, Darlene, was born in Baton Rouge, Louisiana to Horace Sr., and Angie Mae Wellington. She is the oldest of three children. From what I know about my grandfather, my mother loved him greatly. My grandmother, and my mom are best friends. They talk often about any and everything. My grandmother is the reason we ended up in California.

I witnessed a lot of men come into mother's life. None of them stayed around. I longed for just one of them to stay around, even if it was just for me, I was just a desperate little boy who wanted a male's affirmation. I just wanted a man to love me like a son.

I still don't understand, to this day, why my mother was attracted to men that were incarcerated. One of those men gave me my first traumatic experience in my life as a seven-year-old child.

Around age seven or eight I became desensitized to people arguing. One day this became evident, until it became physical. Robert, not his real name, was having an actual fight with my mother. This was the second time; I had seen something like this occur. The first time, I was five. My body froze as I stood there watching my mother get pummeled by this far bigger, stronger, overpowering man who had just recently been released from prison. My brother who is four years younger than me, ran up to him, asking him to stop, and was aggressively shoved to floor. My mother ended up lying motionless, bloody and swollen until the ambulance arrived to haul her to the hospital. Even to this day, I still have no clue who called the ambulance.

When I was nine there was a guy named Kenny, who was also a local barber. He knew a lot of people. He was cool. Him being present was really all I needed as a young boy to deem him a potential candidate for the best "Stand in" for my siblings and me. He would've been a great dad had he stuck around. I was so desperate to have a man around that when arguments did arise, which they always did, I would write notes and make it look like one of my younger siblings had written it, "Are you guys going to break up?" I would write these notes on my large-lined, school paper with my left hand, and simply slide it under the door. Eventually, I would receive an answer, and I would be relieved for the time being. Now that I am older, I realize how much of a desperate kid I was in order to win the acceptance of man who really had no interest in us, but only for my mother's body.

Between 1991 and 1995, three more males came in the picture, but "not in the picture." It was still painful to watch, and I held on to that "Come and go" behavior for a long time. Beginning my ninth-grade year, my mother met a man named Aaron. Up until that point in my life, Aaron may have been the best candidate I had met. He had a daughter who was younger than me, so the fact that he was putting effort into my mother and my siblings at the same time was very refreshing for me. He would take me to school. We would have conversations that I had never had with another adult.

We would do manly activities together that I had never done with anyone before. I felt at peace. I felt that this may be the one for my mother, and more importantly, myself. I still don't know what happened between my mother and Aaron. I never had the heart to ask her, because I honestly didn't want to change my feelings toward him. As a kid you begin to question yourself as if it is your fault. Not too long after their split, he committed suicide leaving behind his daughter. It is safe to say he is the one that got away.

After Aaron there was one final ex-convict that came around, but at this point my heart had hardened towards all men. I already had it in my mind that this man too would use my mother, make all kinds of empty promises, get back on his own feet, and leave. Just as my thoughts predicted, that is exactly what happened.

I was never the child to ever talk back to my mother. When she was angry, yelling, and such, I learned at a young age how to look her in her eyes, appear as if I'm listening, but have a wall up. Every word from her mouth would hit that wall and fall to the floor. I think that would make her angrier sometimes. That was my defense mechanism from childhood that I used throughout my life.

When my mother finally found a man that would stay with her, I was already at the point of being "over" the entire fathering aspect. Knowing what I know about my mother, I don't know why all of these men would come and go. She did any and everything possible to keep them around, from what I observed. You know, the typical domesticity portion of a relationship, but we know that it takes more than that to keep a relationship ongoing.

I was already in my mid-twenties by the time she found a keeper. The good news is he puts up with my mother, and all that is her. He has been there for over ten years now, and it works. I am happy that my mother finally found someone, but there was always a void with me.

I decided at that point to let the search for a father go. I did not start the search for my father until the age of thirty-three, by way of my wife. We will go into this a little later. I did though, still internally hold the hurts and pains of not having a father of my own. The hurts that came along with Aaron were no longer. I can honestly say that I have that inner little boy still lurking that wishes a fatherly relationship was established, but it was meant to be this way. This was the way that God intended.

These insecurities were created for the greater good of my life, and in the life of others. There are countless young individuals, male and female, who are versions of my younger self. They are silently suffering, constantly in emotional distress, putting up walls, and have no clue how to express what they are feeling. That's why I had to go through those things. Do I still have questions? I sure do. Would things have been different if I had a father? Would my life be different? Would the ways that I've made good and bad decisions be different? Would I have been able to channel my emotions better? Would it have taken me so long to accept the love of my wife, my family, or the God that first loved me? These are all questions that are still being answered, even as I write these pages.

These are the insecurities my father created.

CHAPTER 4
I LONGED FOR A RELATIONSHIP

For as long as I can remember, the relationship that I have had with my mother was very shaky. We did not have the typical "television," mother-son relationship. We didn't give hugs daily. We didn't affirm each other. "I love you" wasn't a phrase we used out loud very often, or at all for that matter. I can't remember a time where I simply laid my head on my mother's lap, while she gently caressed my head. These were the actions I longed for as a growing boy, especially from my mother, since she was the only present adult. We have had many up and down years. More down than up. I truly believe it dealt mainly with her age when she birthed me.

She was very young. I was conceived while she was sixteen. She was only seventeen for two months before I was born. My mother was still a kid and was forced to grow up faster than her development. She was placed in a situation to perform adult duties, while still growing into adolescence. Due to this, for the first seven years of my life, I was living with grandparents, my godmother, and my mother. Technically, under these circumstances, it would have been difficult to establish a true relationship with my mother. It has been proven that in the first five years of a child's life, they can learn almost anything. Attachment to the parent is another aspect that comes along with this learning phase. I did not have that early attachment that a child should have with their parents in those years, because I was moving around often.

I knew my mother loved me, but she never said it. We did not actively avoid saying it, it just didn't happen in my family. It was almost like it was taboo. She would buy me certain things that I wanted because that was how she showed me that she loved me. Still, I needed to hear it.

Now that I'm an adult, I think she feels a lot more comfortable expressing herself. But, at thirteen years of age, it was the first time I remember my mother telling me that she loved me, and it wasn't necessarily for the right reason.

In 1985, my grandmother moved to the San Fernando Valley, California from Baton Rouge, Louisiana. My grandfather was mentally, and sometimes physically abusive toward my grandmother. She decided to remove herself from that situation. At the time, I was living with my godmother, Ola Mae, who lived not too far from Baton Rouge. In 1988, my mother came to pick me up, so that we too could relocate to California. We stayed with my grandmother for a few months, before my mother was able to get her own apartment, in the same building. At that point, I began playing football, which became a passion.

Football was the one place I felt like I was someone. I felt like the other parents cared about me as a kid. I started playing football at the age of eight and was actually pretty good. In year thirteen, I played for San Fernando Braves youth football team. One day in the summer, we had a practice that I could not attend for two reasons; I was babysitting my three-year-old sister, and my mother told me to not leave the house.

Football was my passion so on that day I decided to defy her. I rode to practice with one of my childhood friends. My sister, Alveta, was only three at the time and still wasn't completely potty trained. Her being away from the potty for that long wasn't a good idea.

When practice ended, it was almost 10 p.m. My youthful brain hadn't even considered the consequences of my actions as we pulled into my friend's driveway. My baby sister had soaked herself and I was informed that my friend wasn't going to be able to take me home. I only lived about five miles away, but for a thirteen-year old with a urine drenched three-year-old, it was an eternity. I reluctantly called my mother, because now it was beginning to sink in that I would be in some real trouble soon. My hands shook as I dialed the house phone. As I said, "Mama," she instantly began cursing me out. *"Didn't I tell your mother f___ a_____ not to leave this house?! You better get home now!? Where are you at with my baby?!"* I told her that I would just walk home, taking the entire path down Vaughn Street in Pacoima, California.

My sister and I begin walking down the street. I get a few blocks in when I saw a car flying down the street. As the car got closer, I grasp my little sister. The car suddenly stops in the middle of street. My mother jumps out of the passenger side, and storms toward me. As she is cocking her arm back, she yells, "Didn't I tell you not to leave the house?!" She then proceeds to slap all the taste out of my mouth. "Now get in the car," she yells as tears roll down the left side of my numb face.

I quickly go to my room as we arrive back at the house. A few moments later, she came into my room and revealed to me the first time I had heard this phrase. "You know I love you right," she said as she walked by me. I didn't know how to respond because I was angry that she slapped me. A tear rolled down my face, and I internally questioned if that statement were true or not. My conclusion was never determined and seemed to diminish as I grew in young adulthood.

Now as an adult, I realized that I placed my little, three-year sister in jeopardy, having her out at night. I placed myself in jeopardy being a thirteen-year-old boy walking the streets of Pacoima at night. My mother was mostly likely afraid that something bad may have occurred, especially since I was not in the house, as I was requested to be. I am sure if someone had taken my Grace at her age now, and I arrived home without her being present, I may have had the same reaction. My mother was just being a protective, as she should, but at the time, I did not see it that way. I allowed my irrational thirteen-year-old feelings of belonging to cloud the fact that I disobeyed my mother's orders.

One of the lowest points in our relationship and my life came during my freshman year in college. We were not getting along at all. We got in a terrible argument and we didn't speak for a few months. There was also a situation at the same time, where a girl was attracted to me, but I wasn't attracted her. She started a rumor that I was gay. People on campus began to question if I liked women are not, and it began to damage me mentally. No one in my immediate family was aware of any of this. I felt that if I couldn't handle it myself, then I would just let it pass.

One day, I had become fed up with everything that was going on. *"My mother doesn't love me, people think I'm gay, I thought. Why do I even need to be alive?"* One of my uncles had a weapon that I knew of, so I called him to ask him if I could borrow it. "I need to borrow your gun." "Why," he asked. "I have some business I need to handle, and this is the only way that it can be handled." As I am completing my statement, the phone line beeps. I asked my uncle to hold on, and on the other end of the line, is my girlfriend, Tina. She talked me out of making an irrational, emotional decision that would have most likely changed my life, and hers forever . . .

The more I longed for a relationship with my mother, the worst things became. I would occasionally loan my mother money. I would not call it a loan, because when I did give it to her, though she assured she would return it, she never did. I thought of it more as, "I Love her, let me help her out." She is my mother. She did have a job, but being the caregiver for three other children, sometimes a person just needs a little more help. The only problem with lending money to family members is, it would happen too often, and it began to bother me. I was never disrespectful, but I did feel like I was almost being taken advantage of. I just wanted our relationship to be strong.

This one particular time she asked me for an amount that was fairly large, and I gave it to her. But this time I told her that I needed the money back. She replied, "I will give you your money back. Just let me know when you need it." I told her I needed the money at the end of the month.

The time came for me to collect my money, and I let her know. She cursed me out because I asked for the money. Again, I had never asked for any money I let her "borrow," but this one time it was truly necessary. After her tongue lashing, I began to tell her about herself, from feelings that I had felt as a child, up until this point. I was twenty-six when this conversation happened. I did not speak, call, email, or text my mother for the next five years. I was officially done with her, and anything that came along with her. My wife would always urge me to call my mother and apologize. I always refused to follow her wishes.

A few years had passed, and my wife and I were invited to a gospel concert where my friend, Darnel was singing. One song was premised around the emotions of God. It was about how He sees and feels things. Since God made himself flesh, He was able to experience everything that we do, while here on earth. The song was called ***A Heart That Forgives***, by Kevin Levar.

It had gotten to a point in the song where my emotions had overwhelmed me. I thought to myself, "this is how God feels when I do or have done stupid things?" My heart began to metaphorically crumble like I was at a funeral of someone close to me. In that moment, God spoke to me, "you see how you feel right now? This is how I feel when you treat your mother, the way you do."

I had not even thought about my mother for the past four years. The next day, I called her and apologized for the way that I ended our last conversation. I asked her if she could forgive me. This was hard for me. I have been told by countless people that I am stubborn, and very emotional. I have a tendency to hold grudges and be selfish when I feel hurt or rejected. I had to put all pride to the side to make this relationship work.

After that point we began to talk more, and the relationship has changed since that time. I believe that all the wounds she has endured over the years within her life, and the ones that I had, clashed. We both displaced our pains, rejections, and experiences in a selfish way. We were both terrible communicators, but now this lifelong hurt was resolved, because the Holy Spirit brought peace.

If I had sought God earlier, this situation could've been prevented all together.

A Letter To My 14-Year-Old Self:

I am sure you have not had this talk. I know that there is no father in the home, and I have a feeling that your mother does not understand various aspects of raising a young boy who will eventually become a man.

You have to realize that as you grow up, there will be many decisions you will have to make. Every decision you make will have a consequence. The consequences may be good or bad, but there will be one. When you have to make a decision, stop and think about the resulting outcome before making the decision. "Is the decision I am about to

I LONGED FOR A RELATIONSHIP 37

*make, propelling me to be better, or dooming me?"
There can only be one. There is no in-between.*

As you enter high school, you will encounter all types of challenges; both good and bad. Drinking, smoking, having sex, watching pornography, and hanging out with the wrong people are some of the things you don't want to do. Your focus needs to be on making good grades, and excelling in sports, rather than being disrespectful, calling young ladies out of their names, or joining a gang, All of these things will become significant decisions that will propel you to be better or doom you for the rest of your life.

I know you haven't had the type of support that you have longed for all of your life. I know that you were dying to have someone hug you and tell you that they love you and are proud of you. You want someone to come to your sporting events, and kiss you on your forehead when you make good grades.. You need someone to listen to you when you tell them what you are going through. You need them to tell you that you are a handsome young man with beautiful skin and that you are not ugly, but fine!

If only someone would let you know that you are going to be successful in life and encourage you to continue to push through your tasks when you think about giving up.

As you grow into a man, God is going to send you a woman that you are going to push away. I need you to learn that fighting for her will be a huge struggle, but once you get the grasp of that, you will find a good thing.

Though you didn't have a physical father, you will be led and guided through this life with all of your guilts, hurts, and pains. The father that you have longed for, will be a Heavenly one, and He will send people along your journey who are going to help show His love for you. All you will have to do is accept it.

I would understand why it would be difficult for you to believe any of this now because you have lived so long without hearing it. I am going to be that person for you. The Holy Spirit is going to be that person for you. If you ever need to talk, please, I am here for you.

CHAPTER 5
ME . . . KIDS? NEVER!

My wife and I were very late bloomers. We waited thirteen years before we had a child. As I grew into a man, I would always talk about having children, but I was also afraid because I knew absolutely nothing about the process. I think it's just an innate feeling God gives humans. My wife and I were very young when we got married. We eloped because we didn't want anyone to know.

We were both twenty-two. I had just graduated from California State University, Northridge with a degree in Psychology. Tina had another year left before she could graduate. We had discussed early on that we would have two children around twenty-eight years of age. That would give us both time to enjoy each other, learn the game of marriage, travel, and save money to purchase a home. That was the plan, and we were committed. We had a few hiccups along the way, mainly my fault, but the plan was in full motion.

Micheal and Tina

Once my wife and I became one, she instantly got on birth control. The great thing about our marriage is that we did wait until we were married to have sexual relations. I was a skeptic about everything, especially about birth control medication. I felt that it would end up being a major cause of ovarian cancer in my wife. I urged my wife to stop taking birth control medication and we began to use alternative methods.

Fresh out of college, I began working as a behavioral therapist with young children with autism between Pre-K and the first grade. This period in my life gave me a strong desire about having children as my wife and I approached thirty years of age. I was excited, I was ready, I was nervous, I was joyous, and these little children lit my day, every day. I couldn't wait to have my own. After three years of working with these kids, I was hired as a high school teacher in 2007.

At that point, I was nearing the age of twenty-seven. My very first year at my new job, I had the privilege of teaching civics to seniors. Seniors who were already fed up with school, had "senioritis," and could care less about anything governmental that I had to say. You can say that it may have been the worst year of my career, and life. It was so bad that I told my department chair that I would leave if they placed me in another senior class.

At that point, my mind shifted. I was deeply in love with the little children that I worked with previously. I was in love with children that were not even mine. Once I got into the high school ranks, I began to think, "if this is what kids become, I don't want any part of them, EVER!" From that point on, if anyone ever asked when the kids were coming, my response was "Me?! Kids?! NEVER?!" The kids that I taught would even ask, "When are you having kids?" My response was always the same. This was my attitude for the next seven years or so. It appeared that a lot of my "Nevers" were stemming from the kids, but in the back of my mind, now that I am older, I believe I was just displacing my feelings of hurt, not feeling wanted, and rejection on the kids that I was teaching.

I would make very dumb excuses like, "I hate crying and whining," which I did, but what was the real reason I didn't want to ever have kids? A lot of it was me not feeling adequate, not knowing how to be a father, the fear of failing, hoping that my past transgressions wouldn't affect my child as he or she came into the world. It took a lot of breaking down, and opening, for this mindset to change once again. I feel like I was purposefully making myself angry, to never have the want to have children. I would hear the same phrases repeatedly, "You need to have kids." "You would be a great father." I believe all those thoughts and questions plus the my boys from the men's group, were the chisels helping the tip of the iceberg break off.

In 2012 some of my good friends, members of my church as well as my mentors, started a weekly men's meeting to grow and become closer to God. This was a detrimental time in my life for many reasons. First, I had accountability that I never really had. Secondly, I had other men, who were very intimate with God praying for me. Third, it was like a therapy session a lot of the times. On many occasions, I attempted to hold in all anger, shame, and guilt, but the way that the Lord would move in that house, sometimes I would just break down.

My heart had been hardened for many years. Every week, my pastor would pray for me, asking God to love me the way that I always desired, to remove the obstacles that stopped me from accepting His love, and to teach me things about Himself and myself. This was a weekly thing.

After roughly seven years of this ongoing intimate time, I was able to soften my heart, and open to our group about a hurt that I had carried for thirty plus years. It was probably one of the most difficult days during this period. One day I finally decided to open about my feelings for my "biological" father. I had sobbed like a little child. For the first time, that moment revealed there was indeed a father wound that I had suppressed for years.

As I previously mentioned, I moved around a lot as a young kid, from grandmother to godmother to mom. This happened until I was seven years old. As I grew a little older, I heard the story about my biological father. He was apparently an older youth pastor who saw my mother and was attracted to her. My mother told him that she was pregnant, and he urged her not to keep me. He told her that he would leave her if she decided to keep me. She decided, and the rest is history.

Once I was made aware of this story, I instantly grew a hatred for a man I have never seen or spoken to. The first time I cried in front of my mother, I was fifteen years old. We were talking, because I was extremely upset of the different men that I would observe coming in and out her life, as well as mine. I was selfish. I longed for even the idea of a father, and never had it. It was a moment unprovoked because my brokenness has reached its peak.

I told this story for the first time in my early thirties, and I truly believe this was the start of my emotional fatherless breakthrough. This was eventually going to open the door for something greater in the future.

After years of praying, opening, trying to submit myself to Christ, I revealed this suppressed pain, and it turned my "Never" into, "if that is what God wants?" I still had my "never" foot in the door, but the door was beginning to close behind me. One day in 2015, while at school, a few kids were sitting in my classroom before school began, as they always did. My room was the hangout spot for all my athletes. The topic of children came up. "Welly, (short for my last name, Wellington), we know you don't want children, but if you did, would you want, a boy or girl?" I still didn't want to say, "Yes, I want children," but I answered the question truthfully, and from my heart.

"I really wouldn't mind if I had a boy or girl. If I had a boy, I would love him just as hard, but if I had a girl . . . I would show her the way that a man is supposed to treat a woman. She would know without a shadow of doubt that I love her, and she will understand early what a relationship should really look like. She will know a love that only a father can give her."

At that point one of the girls in the room began balling as the bell rang for first period. She walked over to my desk and dropped her head unto my shoulder. While balling like a baby she blurted out, "Why doesn't he love me?" She was referring to her father. I didn't know what to do at the time, so all I could do is give her a hug. I felt all her pain as she cried harder once I embraced her. The pain she felt was the pain I was holding in for thirty plus years. That was truly another turning point for me, regarding my mindset towards children. I would never want my child to experience that type of emotional pain, and sense of rejection that I, as well as my student, had experience at critical points in our lives. I know that there are millions that feel the same way. There are probably millions of "Me's" walking around. I have been working with children, ages three to eighteen, for more than twenty years. I truly believe that God allowed me to go through the pain of being fatherless, experiencing what it means to be rejected, and learn from it, so that I could be what every kid I work with needs. I also believe He wanted to show me that though I didn't have an earthly father, He was there. He placed situations and people in my life to get me to draw to Him, so that He could show me. If I had not gone through that period in my life, I could not be used to fill the voids of other kids who may be experiencing the same thing. Play it forward, and they will also.

CHAPTER 6
IF YOU LOVE ME, THEN WHY?

Going into college I wanted to graduate in four years. The lead speaker at the athlete orientation mentioned that the average athlete graduated in six years, but I wanted to complete my eligibility, start graduate school, and begin my career as a teacher. I also wanted to find my wife in college. Those were my goals, and I was going to reach them.

When I met Tina, we didn't officially meet. It was more like several different situations of us coming across each other. Because of my goals, I was laser focused on school. One day I was sitting against a wall, waiting for my class to begin, and I hear a voice say, "hey Tyrese." I look up, and there is this young woman sitting and smiling, moving her head side to side like a bobble head doll. I just brushed it off.

I didn't notice this until later, but during class, she would always come up to the person sitting behind me to ask them a question. Later, she revealed that in those times, she was trying to get my attention. Again, I was laser focused on graduating in four years.

Now remember, we still haven't officially met, but the first day I noticed her, she had her hair pulled back into a ponytail. I love ponytails and corn rows. I was walking to my dorm from class, which she didn't attend that day. She was walking toward me, and I was nervous. I thought she was cute.

She approached me and asked, "Do you have the homework?" I said yes, and we both continued our ways. We continued to see each other around campus and in class, but at this point I was intimidated to approach her because I really had no game. None. I wouldn't know how to approach a woman. A lot of that was insecurity. The first time I worked up the nerve to speak to her, I did a horrible job.

We both joined the California State Northridge Black Student Union Choir, so we would meet at the Black

House for practices. Her hair was corn rolled this day, and I walked over to her and said, "Your hair looks better that way."

"What do you mean, my hair looks better this way?" she responded.

This probably was not the best way to spark up a conversation. The insecurities that I had in myself, and based on things that I had learned, I displaced those insecurities onto her, and we were starting on a bad note. Side note, and I had no clue of this situation until later, but one of my childhood friends, before Tina and I had a single conversation together, told her that I was going to be her husband. A few months later with the help of my friend Aaron, he asked her to be my girlfriend for me.

"He needs to come talk to me himself," she said.

After we began officially dating I realized early on that she was different. She was not like any other woman I had ever met. It was scary, but I wanted to keep her around because of how she was. Our relation wasn't the greatest. She was ideal, and I was messed up. She attempted to show me what it meant for a person to care about their significant other, and I simply pushed her away. I have no clue why she stayed with me. She was young, pretty, educated, and there were other guys attracted to her. Why choose a hard-headed, insecure, stubborn boy like me. I guess God had a different plan for both of us.

Insecurities controlled me for a large portion of the early part of our courting period. The girls I liked, I never heard anything positive from them, so to hear Tina saying, "you're the most beautiful man I've ever seen. I love you," was difficult for me to believe or accept.

I would refute every positive thing she would tell me. "That's not true. You don't love me. No one tells me that they love me." This was an ongoing situation for years of us dating, and especially into the early stages our marriage.

In spite of the shakiness of our relationship, two and a half years into us dating, I asked her to marry me. Though Tina said yes, later she told me that she didn't think we were ready. She wanted to say no. As I have grown, I began to agree with her; we weren't ready for marriage.

There were many things I needed to change about myself. There were things in me that needed to be broken, and I was too dumb at the time to face them. There are still times where I allow these mindsets to surface. I am still a work in progress. But, on September 6, 2003, which was five days after Tina's birthday, we eloped in my former pastor's office with two witnesses that we knew would not tell a soul. We did not want anyone to know about our marriage.

Neither one of us believed anyone in our families wanted us to get married. We were young and I was immature. We never asked for anyone's approval of our marriage, we just did it.

We made our pastor aware of this desire beforehand and yet he announced it at church the very next day. We never asked him why he revealed this confidential information. We simply brushed it off, but there was a lot of backfire from it. We had a lot of people angry at us. My Aunt still brings up this situation, even now, sixteen years later.

The first several months of our marriage were very shaky, and it was all because of me. Tina was literally the ideal wife. She loved God, affirmed me, though I still wasn't accepting it; cook, clean, and help me save money. God. She was all that anyone could ask for in a wife.

Because we waited until we were married to have sex, that was great too. It was literally taking place three to four nights a week. Who could ask for anything more? Well, a person with low self-esteem would.

I rarely went out before I was married, but as soon as I became married, I began going out more than I ever had. I started to receive attention from women that wouldn't have given me the time a day before. I revealed this to my wife, and I told her that I enjoyed the attention. Granted, she was giving me the same attention at home. We had a long argument about this. I was a very stubborn, childish boy, who would deflect my wrong doings on her to make it appear as if she was in the wrong.

Three months after we were married, she told me that she had a Christmas concert that she was singing in and told me that she wanted me to be there to see her. I told her I would, and when the time came to be there, my friends told me that they were going out that night. I told her that I was not going to her concert, but I was going to go out with my friends instead. That statement infuriated her.

"I waited twenty-two years to give myself to someone, and you are telling me that you like getting compliments from other girls? You take my virginity, and you would rather go to the club and party, instead of watching me sing?!"

I was quiet and ignored her as I typically did when we were arguing. As I was sitting on the couch, she jumped on my lap, and slapped me multiple times. I roughly picked her up and moved her to the side, so I could leave. She blocked the door. I asked her nicely to move so that I could go and cool off. She insisted that I stay. This continued for about ten minutes. At that point, I picked her up, sat her on the couch, and ran out the door. She ran behind me, yelling that I stay. I ran all the way to the dorms, which are about eight hundred meters away, without looking back.

I called my cousin to come pick me up, and I did not go back for about a month. Halfway through the month we met with a couple who did counseling at our church at the time. We revealed the situation, but I was done mentally.

My mindset was, if I put my hands on her, I would be in prison. I did provoke it, but that doesn't justify the result. I decided to stay at my aunt's house until I decided what I was going to do. Even in my anger I knew that I wanted to be with Tina forever, but my pride, my insecurities, my lack of guidance, and curiosities caused me to remain away longer.

I put myself in a very bad situation. One night the same week that I left we decided to go to a jazz club for young adults. I was literally there to enjoy some good adult music with my boys. The entire time there was this woman staring at me through the mirror that was behind our table. At first, I thought there was something behind us but realized she was looking at me.

After the show ended, she and her friends decided to come over to our table and engage in small talk. The talk continued all the way to our cars. I was driving because my friends had a few drinks at the club. The girl and her friends pulled up alongside the truck and placed her hand outside of the window. She said, "before I give you my number, do you have a girlfriend, or are you married?" I was at a crossroads. In my mind, in that split second, I was having a full-blown conversation with myself.

Yes, you are married, so say that you are married. Yes, you are married, but your wife put her hands on you. No, you are not married. You are technically separated now. Take her number. It is not going to go that far. See how far you can take it without going too far. My inner voice convinced me to respond.

"No, I'm not married," I said as she handed me her number. Her name was Melissa. We spoke on the phone for about a week. At the end of the week, I revealed that my cousin had a football game in San Jose, California on that Saturday. "I have a cousin that lives in San Jose. We can go out there too." Melissa and her friend wound up driving to San Jose. I rode up with her as we followed my uncle's Suburban to our destination.

I never understood the phrase "you can't have your cake and eat it too." Still I felt the conviction of what I was doing. "But, I'm mad at Tina," I said to myself.

Later that night after the game, we went back to my cousin's hotel, just to chill. She sat on my lap, and we were talking, and she kissed my cheek, and slowly got to my lips, and we began kissing. That is as far as it went, as my convictions got worse. I pretended that I had to go to the restroom, because as my thoughts raced just like before she asked if I were married. This was as far as it would go. We still spoke after that, but it was very awkward, and it was almost as if after, that we hated each other.

It had been about five weeks and I hadn't been home or spoken to Tina. She knew of the month-long fling that I had with this young lady. Melissa called my home one particular day, and her and Tina spoke over the phone. The disgust she had for me carried over for the next several years. I tried as hard as I could to prove that it wouldn't happen again, but as the saying goes, "Hell hath no fury like a woman scorned." I scorned my wife for a situation I started. I dug myself into a deeper hole and shoveled the dirt onto my own head.

Divorce was a word that I threw around much too freely. Every time a problem would arise, instead of facing it, which

I wasn't used to, I would always throw out the D-word. My mechanism was to "cut off," not fight. I am not justifying my actions, but I did not know how to fight for my marriage. I was afraid to lose her but had no clue how to keep her around. I did not have the experience, guidance, nor an example of what the statement "for better or for worse, until death do you part," really meant. My escape would be to entertain past women on the internet, in which I knew I shouldn't have been doing. They were my ego boosters, and fueled my own anger, making me more infuriated. Boy, was I stupid!

The only way things were able to be turned around is through our desire to be closer to Christ. The Holy Spirit, and Him alone has to breakdown the deeply rooted things in us, but mainly me. I wanted to be the epitome of Ephesians 5, "husbands, love your wives as Christ loved the church. Lay down your lives for them. Wives submit to your husbands as unto the Lord."

After the terrible years that we experienced, I realized meeting Tina was the best thing that had happened to me, and I had to change my actions so I could keep her. I had to acknowledge what she meant to me, understand how she helped me in my growth as a man, and how to love her. Praying for a true physical change in me was a daily process and still is. My daily prayer was to remove anything that's in me that's not pleasing to God. I asked Christ to search and help me to be the man He had designed and purposed me to be, so I could be the husband for Tina. I vowed that no matter how bad things became, I would never use the word, divorce again. I had to learn to fight for what mattered and stop running from my self-inflicted wounds.

Tina has forgiven me for what I have mentally and emotionally put her through, but she too had to endure an ongoing healing process. She now says it as a joke, when we tell the story, but she has said that our married began a few years ago, though we've been married sixteen years. We are living this thing out the way that God intended it to be. I am not saying it is easy, but it all comes down to making a choice. Do you want it, or do you not?

It is now evident that none of this was even remotely be possible without the Holy Spirit. We are beings that have our own opinions, ideologies and feelings. Those things often get in the way of the bigger picture. My good friend Dr. Plunkett has a prayer that he says often, as do I, "help me to love my wife as You love her. Let me see her through Your eyes." Difficult task? Yes. But with the Holy Spirit, we can do all things through Christ who strengthens us.

CHAPTER 7
YOU ARE NOT THE FATHER

For thirty-three years of my life, I had only known one story about my biological father. His name was Willie. He was a little older than my mother. The story of the way my biological father left instilled hatred, anger, sense of rejection, pain, and any other verb that describes heartache. I felt this way for years.

One shocking day that all changed. In 2014, just before turning thirty-three years of age, my mother calls me out of the blue. "I need you to call this man. His name is Mr. Jackson. He was trying to get in contact with me for thirty years, to try and find you. He has been looking for you for thirty years. He has believed this entire time that you are his son."

At this point I am confused. I become quiet for a moment. "Wait a minute. I don't understand. What are you talking about? What about the guy that I've known about this entire time?"

"I will explain later. Here is his number. Call him as soon as we get off the phone and call me back," she said.

To say that I was nervous while I dialed his number would be an understatement. My palms were sweating, I was perspiring through my shirt, and I hardly ever sweat.

I was terrified.

As the phone rang, my wife, just as anxious as me, urged me to place the cell phone on the speaker. She had always wanted me to attempt to find my biological father. I would always brush her off because I didn't want to find him. If I saw him, I may have broken his entire face. "Hello," he said with a slight, southern drawl.

"Hello, Sir. My name is Micheal Wellington, and I am Darlene's son. She told me you were looking for me."

"Yeah man, I've been looking for you for thirty years. I've always thought you were my son."

At this point I am super confused, but at the same time almost relieved. A slight smirk pushed through my cheeks as he spoke. The hurt, anger, and pain that had felt for so long had dissipated in the matter of 5 seconds.

"I have never heard about you," I explained. "You were never part of the story that I had known my entire life. The story I was told for thirty years was about a man named Willie. Willie was a youth pastor who was a little older than my mother. According to the story, Willie impregnated my mother at sixteen. She proceeded to reveal this information to him once she found out. He then told my mother that he could not have a child this young in his life. The sentence that replays over and over in my mind, which helped create the anger in me is this, "If you don't have an abortion, I'm leaving you." This story didn't involve a Mr. Jackson.

Mr. Jackson continued. "With all the kids I've had, I would always get sick when their mothers were pregnant. This was usually how I knew my partner was pregnant." I would be one of five children of his if this were a true statement. "One day I got real sick. I approached your mother and asked her if she was pregnant. She must have been mad at me for some reason, because her response was 'No, I'm not pregnant, and even if I was, it's not yours." Even after she told me that, I still believed that you were my son. I always have."

I became very quiet. I didn't say a single word for the next few minutes. In the back of my mind, I was wondering why my mother never told me this story. Why would she leave something so critical a secret for thirty-three years?

"You still there," he asked.

"Yeah, I am," I replied. "There is just a whole lot going through my mind now. This is all new to me."

"I am still really good friends with the people that lived across the street from you guys on Sussex Avenue," he said. This is where I lived partially for seven years of my life. "One day I asked my boy if he could somehow get in touch with your mama and he did. He gave me the number, and I called."

I was still silent because I was blown away at this point. He continued.

"So, I needed to contact you, because I knew after all this time, you were my son. I would like to start a relationship with you now. I know that it has been a long time, but we can start from now."

I told him that I was still confused, because the story I had known my whole life, was either a lie, or the information about Mr. Jackson was withheld. After about an hour into the conversation, he told me he would call me every day until we got to know each other. My wife is now staring at me like a little kid who is trying to get their parents attention.

As soon as the call ended, I called my mother. "Who is Mr. Jackson?" I received a half story about the situation, but she did mention the "I am not pregnant, but if I was," part.

"Why would you say that, if you were indeed pregnant," I asked.

"I was mad at him, because I felt that he liked one of my friends from across the street. He was always over there," she responded.

"So, you allowed me to suffer with anger, pain, rejection, and any other verb that means hurt for thirty-three years, because you felt he liked another woman," I asked. Again, I got silent. Then she said her favorite line.

"The past is the past. Get to know him. He has been looking for you, for a very long time." I thought about it for a few hours, talked about it with my wife, and decided, why not. What's the worst thing that could happen?

From the months of February to June we spoke on the phone almost every day, about little things. I truly believe that God ordained this meeting, because every time we spoke, something would happen to my heart. It softened. Day by day, and week by week, I started to fall in love with the man who revealed he had been in search of me for thirty years. The neglected, hurt, pained, fearful little boy had a person in search for him for thirty years. I felt wanted for only the second time in my life, behind my wife.

Every time we spoke, the wall of hate continued to fall. The wall that I set up toward a person that I had hated, though I'd never met him, began to come down because of Mr. Jackson. In July of that same year, my sister was going to be receiving her master's degree, and we decided we would drive to Texas to attend the ceremony. I told Mr. Jackson and he said, "you and your wife should come here too, so that we can formally meet." I ended up staying in the South for an extra week, for the meeting.

On a Thursday, my wife Tina and I hopped in the car to take a five-hour trip to from Dallas, Texas to Zachery, Louisiana. I was so nervous that my foot was heavy on the gas. I believe divine intervention took us all the way to Louisiana, because I was driving eighty-five miles per hour the entire trip, and there were no highway patrol officers in sight.

As I drove through Louisiana, I was amazed at the greenery. I was actually trying to take my mind off the extreme nervousness that began to overtake my body. I drove over a bridge heading into Baton Rouge, where I grew up, as I continued on my way to Zachery. I turned the corner, heading down the final street to my destination, and my heart began to pound as I drew closer. The GPS states, "you have reached your destination."

As I am driving up, I see him getting out of his Ford 150 vehicle in the driveway. My eyes began to tear up, but I didn't want to look soft in front of my wife. As we get out of the car, I greeted him with a handshake, but he pulled me in for a hug. We sat and talked alone for a few hours, and we were also allowed to stay in his home for the weekend. I met his wife and two daughters, but it wasn't the best of meetings. There were a few things said by the wife, and one of the daughters that didn't sit well with me, but I wouldn't allow it to affect me as much. I just remained quiet while those things were being said.

"You don't look anything like us. You are dark-skinned, and we are light-skinned. Why would someone wait until they are a grown man to find their dad?" All of these things were being said right in front of me, but I never responded. In my mind, I responded, angrily. *I shouldn't look like you because you guys are not my father. I didn't wait to find anyone; he was looking for me. I bet you didn't know that?!* All of these thoughts were playing over and over in my mind as they were talking. My wife mentioned, if we were not in their home, she would've let them have it.

That really did something to me on that weekend, but I kept my mind on the real reason I was in Zachery, Louisiana; to meet the man that had been looking for me for the last thirty plus years of my life. The last physical encounter we had, he hugged me, kissed me on my cheek and said, "No matter what happens here, I still am your father, and I will always love you." Those words were internalized as I left heading back to Dallas.

I continued to speak with Mr. Jackson on a regular basis, but what was said at the dinner table at his home had bothered me to the core. The way that my mind is, something can replay over and over for weeks, and sometimes months, if it bothers me. I did not tell him this, but because it was so heavy on my heart, I asked if we could take a DNA test, and I would pay for it. One reason was to make true of what he thought, and what I hoped. The other reason was to prove his wife wrong.

The DNA test finally arrived, but I was a little confused. In the package there was a swab, and a paper envelope, and that was all that was within the package. I thought there should at least be a plastic envelope, so that the DNA is not tainted as it is shipped back to the institution. I swabbed my mouth and placed it within the paper envelope that was meant to send back the items, but the moisture from the saliva was seeping through. I was extremely skeptical after this, so the next day I called the company, and revealed the situation. They stated that no matter what I believe about their system, it is one hundred percent accurate. At that point I couldn't do anything expect hope for the best.

Though I knew it would take at least three weeks before the results were available, I checked every day. It was almost obsessive. It was an addiction, as I would check two or three times a day. During a block day, where each class period is held longer, on a Wednesday, a few weeks later, it was a gloomy day. It was slightly drizzling, and the bell had rung for nutrition. I typically go to the teacher's cafeteria to eat breakfast, but my addiction to know the truth had gotten the best of me. I was starving, but my anxiety covered my hunger. There was about a minute left before class was scheduled to begin, and as I finally logged on, palms sweating, heart pounding, the results were in.

"There is a ZERO percent chance that Mr. Jackson is your father." It was set up like a movie.

I read the results over and over, as if the words would change. Maybe I read it wrong.

My heart dropped, my eyes began to heavily water, and if I would have blinked, I would have started balling. My third period class walked in as I was reading the results, and they instantly knew something was wrong. I am usually the cheery teacher, but I was definitely not myself on this day. The students asked if I were okay, and truthfully, I replied, "No, I'm not, but life goes on."

After those results came in my passion to speak with Mr. Jackson diminished. I called him here and there, but that void that I thought was filled was not. The good that came out of this situation was the hatred that had been built up for so many years, had been broken.

I am still uncertain who my biological father is, and it does bother me, but not as much as it did in the past. I believe God allowed Mr. Jackson to find me to break the hardness that had been created in me for so many years. I still talk to him today, but it isn't as frequent as it was when we first began to speak.

CHAPTER 8
SURRENDER IT ALL TO ME

I had a major problem totally surrendering my everything to God. I would surrender certain things to Him, but some things I wanted to hold on to. I didn't want to surrender to God, and His will end up being different than what I had set up for myself. I did not want to become angry at Him. My mindset was focused on doing as much as possible without God's help. So, if I did things on my own, I could only be upset with myself when things turned out wrong.

At times, this was an ongoing cycle in different parts of my life. I thought not trusting God was safe. I liked being safe. I'm not Peter. I'm not Abraham. I'm not Noah. I'm not David. My faith wasn't strong enough then to know that God will do what His Word says. How do I trust all the way in a

God that I can't see, especially when I have had a lifetime of not trusting anyone? Now, all doubt is gone.

However, I still fall short in this area at times with God as well as people. On the flip side I can say my trust has increased greatly from what it was in the past. God has shown me on many occasions that He is with me. He will never leave me. All things are possible, if I believe it. He has also taught me see the good in people, because that is what He does. He sees the finished product.

God is the all-knowing, all seeing, all loving Father. His Will for our lives is perfect. He knows all things, positive or negative, what we're going to engage in before we were formed in our mother's womb. He will never leave nor forsake us. So, why is it so difficult to submit our everything to Him?

With me, it is an internal and physical conflict. Not having an earthly father made it extremely hard to submit to a Heavenly Father. If I never trusted a male who was supposed to nourish me, affirm me, teach me, guide me, help me discipline me, cover me, and most importantly love me, how then would I be able to trust the Father of all? This was my struggle, and sometimes it still rears its head in certain situations.

I struggle with this when it comes to "asking" God for things. I am not really big on asking for things. I refuse to to treat God like a genie in a bottle. My attitude was, "If it happens, it happens. If it does not, it does not." That was my mechanism for a long time. It was my way of not feeling the rejection that comes along when God says no, or not at this time. In every instance, it would bring up all those feelings of being rejected by my earthly father.

When it came time to have a child, I absolutely did not want to have any. This is one of those areas that I did not want to surrender. "But the word says be fruitful and multiply (Genesis 1:28)." My response to that was always, "well the earth is fruitful now. It doesn't need to be filled anymore. God was not talking to me when he made that declaration." I fought this for so long.

As I mentioned earlier, I joined a men's group with a few guys from my church. The conversation about kids would always come up with me. I would block it every time, like Dikembe Mutombo, a 7.2" former professional basketball player known for blocking shots. "I do not want to hear that! I do not want you to pray for that! I do not want to talk about that!"

About four years had passed since the men's group was created. This was around the same year that I was introduced to Mr. Jackson and met his family. My hardened heart started to soften, and my speech began to change. I went from saying never to, if God wants us to have children, we will. My foot was still in the door of "never," mentally. In December of 2015 my wife and I were going to my mother's house in Texas for the holidays. A few days before, we attended a church that her aunt's husband pastored. We only went to the church to send off her cousin who was moving to Chicago to start medical school. It turned out to be something else.

At this point in our relationship, my wife and I began praying about kids, and our answer was quickly approaching at the church service, and we didn't know. My wife's aunt had an ex-husband who held a job in the FBI and could find information on any person in the United States. Apparently early in our relationship, they did a background check on me to make sure I wasn't a lunatic. They found one child with my exact name in Louisiana, that had been taken from his family at a young age, because someone in the child's life threw him in a boiling tub of water trying to kill him. I am not sure if that happened to me, but I get it. From that story, they concluded that Tina hadn't gotten pregnant yet, because I had a problem producing sperm, due to the tub incident. The Aunt revealed this to her current husband. This story still makes me laugh to this day. What they didn't know, was that my wife and I were using the "pull-out method" for the last twelve years, because we did not want to have children.

As the church service was ending, it was time for alter call. The pastor called for the people to come to the altar, and not one person walked up. He waited a little while longer, then called me to come forward. In my mind, I thought, I don't want to go up there. *The Holy Spirit didn't push me to go up there.* I shook my head, saying, "no." He called again, and the twelve people that were present turned to look at me. I had to go now. Then he called for my wife to also come up.

I took a deep breath, closed my eyes, and began to pray silently, before he started. "Lord if this is your will give me peace, and let these words be yes, and amen." He then placed his hand in between my lower abdomen, and bladder, and began to pray for the removal of the problems I have there. I literally laughed out loud as he said it, because I had just been made aware of the bathtub story. *I HAVE NO PROBLEM*, I said in my head. He then placed his hand on my wife's stomach, and in the middle of his prayer, he called her Sarah. "No more barrenness, Sarah," he said as we both laughed. In the Bible Sarah was unable to bear a son for Abraham for years. Now I'm thinking, "Is this a joke?!" As we finished, I had a lot of thoughts in my mind, but I was at peace at the same time.

The following week we arrived at my mother's house. She is a foster parent and in this particular season she had this three-month-old little boy, whom I truly believe I fell in love with in the two weeks we were in Texas. He would cry, I would pick him up. I would rock him in my arms and would fall asleep. One day he was crying, and I walked in the house, and as I began to speak, he instantly stopped. Though I wasn't his father, the child knew the sound of my voice. I think that moment did it for me.

Eventually he was taken back by his original birth family. I believe the time he was with my mother I was supposed to meet him.

December 28th, we returned home. We had not been intimate for about three weeks, because we had a feeling this was going to be it. We sat and talked for a while before we started to caress and kiss one another. "If it is God's will, if He wants this, we will surrender to him." For the first time in twelve years, we concluded our intimate encounter in the way that it is designed to be concluded. I laid there for a couple minutes, and I said, "That may be the one."

Five weeks had passed. I had known from the start that she was pregnant. She did not want to believe she was. I told her to take a home test. I was shaking and waiting by the door as she went into the bathroom.

"The positive means I am not pregnant right," she asked from the other side of the door. Tina did end up being pregnant that day. We instantly set up an appointment for her to see a doctor where they assured what we already knew. I was scared. I was happy. I was unsure of the future. There were many things going through my mind at this time.

Micheal and Grace Michelle

Surrendering your will to God's is always hard, but it is simple at the same time. Our experiences, heartaches, rejections, and disappointments hinder us from submitting. Once you do, you will realize that it was all worth it.

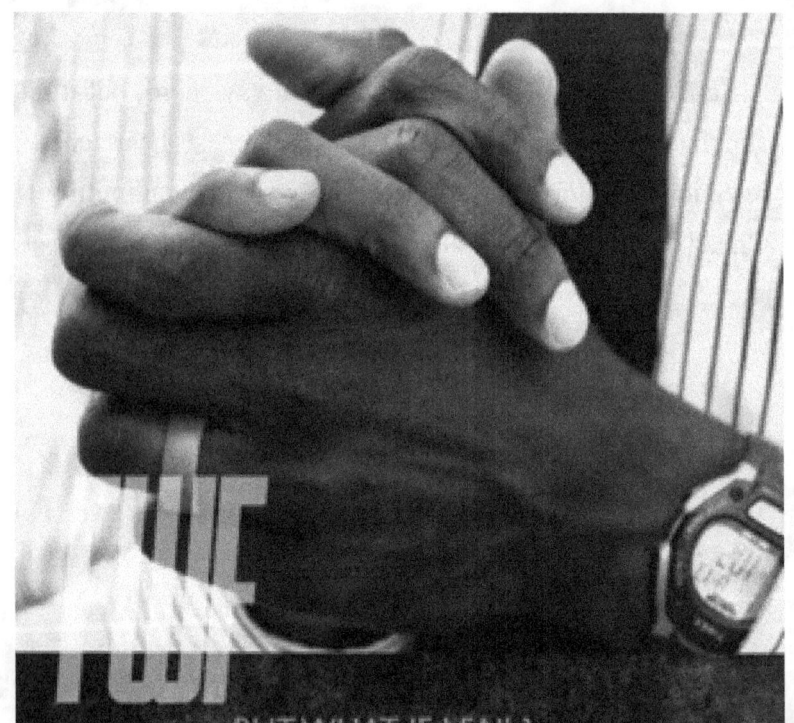

CHAPTER 9
LET ME LOVE YOU

In 2014, a year before my wife was pregnant, I was still on the fence about ever having kids. I was still saying "no," but it was a lot softer as we approached the possibility.

I am a dreamer. I have very vivid dreams. Some of my dreams are so real, it is as if my eyes are open and I am seeing them in 3D. One night I was asleep in my bed and I woke up to two heart-piercing, very loud, crying babies. I walked over to the crib that was in our room, and in it were two little twin girls. Why was I having a dream about twins? As I walked over to the cribs the little girls both have names under their bodies. The little girl to the left's name was Grace Michelle. The little one to the right was named Glory Belle. Grace means Gods unwarranted favor. Michelle means one who is like God. Glory means magnificent. Belle means beautiful. I was blown away by this dream, but once the pregnancy happened, I already knew the name of my first child.

You can learn a lot about your relationship with the Holy Spirit when you have children. Many different nuances come out of this experience. You will learn so much about yourself and about God as you continue to experience parenthood.

When my wife officially found out she was pregnant, my entire demeanor changed. I was doing everything that she asked at the drop of a dime. I would rub her stomach, her feet, her head until she fell asleep snoring. I was preparing for a new addition which I would now have to also love unconditionally.

But, you don't know how to be a father. You didn't have one. You have no clue how to do this. But what if I fail? What if you don't have enough money to take care of her. What if, What if, What if? The Lord was working on me in this process. Trust me. This was the one phrase that constantly played in my mind the entire time. "Take no thought for your life" (Matthew 6:25).

My wife was about seven months pregnant. We were lying in bed as I was rubbing her stomach. I began singing to the future Grace Michelle Wellington, and my emotions took over. I was singing ***Holy Spirit, You are Welcome Here***, by Kim Walker. I believe all the thoughts I initially had about being a father rushed through my head, and I began sobbing. *What is going on?* I stopped singing. "No, don't stop," my wife urged me to continue, as she was also enjoying the serenade. She always told me to use my voice. I like to keep a lot of my emotions and words closed to myself. Typically, when I would sing, I would hum. I felt more comfortable this way. Again, that rejection and "Not good enough" aspect would always present itself.

Once my daughter was born on September 16, 2016, it was a very different experience. I wanted to love her from a place that I was hurting. I didn't hear "I Love You" very often, so I would tell her a million times a day. I wasn't kissed very much as a child, so I kissed her little chubby cheeks every moment I had. I would sing to her until she fell asleep. I would caress her little head and lay her on my chest. I wanted to do everything possible, even as an infant, to let her know I would never leave her. I would never have her second guessing whether I loved her.

I love it when my daughter stares at me. It is only on a particular occasion. Now don't get me wrong, I know that there is a strong "mother-daughter, I carried you nine months," type of connection, but my daughter would only make eye contact with me when I sang to her. No matter the situation with my wife, Grace would always look in her eyes. Even as a grown man, I believe that would uprooted feeling of rejection that were still lingering within me.

During Grace's third month, one day I was trying to rock her to sleep. I was walking around the living room. I was singing to her, and she still wouldn't look at me. She always looks at me when I sing to her. At this point rejection was in my face. I was feeling things that I felt as a child. My heart was almost hurting because my daughter would not even turn her little head to glance at me. I tried to sing better; make the notes a little more smoother. I tried to turn her body to look at me. I tried all that I could, to get her to look me in the eyes. Though she was an infant, it is almost felt to me as if she was purposefully trying not to look at me. I think a little bit of that stubbornness came from me.

In the silence of my mind I said, *Why will you not look at me?* As I finished my statement, the Holy Spirit spoke to me very clearly and said, "Why will you not look at me?" My eyes began to tear up.

This is the same way that our Father wants us to lean on Him, cling to Him, trust in Him, call on Him, spend time with Him, and look at Him. He is waiting, but just as my daughter pridefully looked away from me as I demanded her attention, we behave the same way to our Heavenly Father.

I was so happy when my daughter was an infant. She couldn't move. She couldn't say no. She would simply lie there and had to deal with mommy and daddy kissing her cheeks all day. As she got older, and started to become more mobile, she started to push us away. Once she began talking and moving, she could say "no more kisses, Dada," to me. She would also straight arm me like the late, great, Chicago Bears' running back, Walter Payton, would deliver to slow, would-be tacklers.

Even as an adult man who must raise a daughter, her telling me no, just in me wanting to love on her, would bring up feelings of rejection. Why would she not want this? This is what I wanted. What I did notice about her, is she would not want me close, but wanted me close, at the same time. She would tell me "no kisses," and push me away, and turn her body away from me. Then she would, while facing the other direction, place her little hand on me, as to say," I still want you close."

Micheal, Tina, and Grace Michelle

This is also how we treat God. "I want to do this by myself. Your will is perfect, just not perfect for me. I want to be close, but not to the point where it hurts."

She is still growing, and I am learning that her name has a lot to do with my relationship with her and my relationship with Christ. Her name is Grace. Grace is something that God gives us every single day that we wake up to see the sun. Every day that we sin, HIS grace is enough to allow us to come back to Him. It is His grace by which we are saved from damnation. It is His Grace that softened my heart, so that I could experience His love through Grace. With my daughter, I have to understand that she is a toddler. She will bring up emotions in me, due to her child-like actions. She is a child that is learning her own way, and all I have to do is be her father. I need to care, comfort, teach, love, and guide her, as she learns herself, and how this world operates.

Since affirmation is something that should be committed to often and early, I affirm my daughter daily with five phrases that she should know and take with her, the rest of her life. "I am fearfully and wonderfully made. I am beautiful.

I am smart. I am loved. I am special." You must affirm your own children, because if you don't, someone else will. Even in her young age, she has begun to blossom in her toddler years. Grace loves the show Peppa Pig. She has a bunch of toys that correspond with the show. One day we were playing together, she grabbed George (Peppa's little brother), and said "George, you are fearfully and wonderfully made." I almost teared up.

I am aware that often life becomes difficult. This causes some men and women to abandon their children. In the end, it is only the child that suffers. Looking at my daughter daily reminds me of the deep-rooted hurts and pains that my inner child still harbored towards my biological father. The difference now is that there are no longer any more feelings of anger, but "why?" How could someone have a child and then abandon it? How could you blame my mother for so much? If you would've been around, things may have been different. We all know that I would not be who I am today without these situations, but they were always thoughts. It was meant to be this way.

One day while at church my daughter was sitting on my lap, and I was praying. I was holding her, kissing the top of her head, and rocking back and forth. In that moment I was just trying to hear from the Holy Spirit. Suddenly a song by Leon Timbo called "Abba" begins to play on the television. Abba means "Father" in Hebrew. I had never heard the song, so I was really attentively listening to the lyrics. *"Your Thoughts define me, You're inside of me, You-are-my-reality."* That hit home. All of the things I had allowed to define me for years were all lies, but I believed them to the core.

The part that broke me all the way down was, *"Daddy when you move, I want to walk in, what may look like Your shadow, when you move. The way you love, I want to get past all the hurts and pains of my life, Daddy I want to love. I want to take myself, and I want to fit it in Your shoes, Daddy can I put my foot in Your shoes? Daddy, can I lay my head in Your lap, because you know I am crying before I shed a tear. Daddy I just want to say I love You. Daddy I just want to say thank You for never leaving, never leaving me."*

Like a soda can that has been shaken, everything that I had held in exploded out, and at that moment I began to cry out loud. This was the hard cry, with snot coming from my nose and everything. It was as if every negative emotion I had ever held toward my mother, my biological father, and the guilt from the devastating things I've done in my life all came out at the same time. It was like a cry that I had never experienced, one that had been bottled up, for almost four decades.

As I wailed, I squeezed my little Grace as hard as her little body would allow. I would never want her to feel what I had felt as I released that cry. She somehow wiggled out of my arms, only to turn around, facing me on my lap. She placed both of her little hands on my cheeks, looked me in my eyes, and said "I love you Dada," in the softest voice. This made my tears come down harder. I knew for a fact at that moment, that the one living God really did love me, and He sent my baby Grace to show me in the flesh. My saving Grace.

Though it may not always appear to be that way, the Father loves us. There is absolutely nothing we can do to be separated from it. We sin and fall short every single day, but as King David said, "Even if I make my own bed in hell, He is with me" (Psalm 139:8). I think that day, I may have been truly liberated from the thoughts of fear, rejection, not being wanted, guilt, and everything else, that kept me mentally bound for so long.

CHAPTER 10
DOES GOD REALLY FORGIVE?

I have forgiven different people in my life. I had to forgive my mother, my father, and other people. It was easy as I grew older to forgive all the things that I had experienced. It has, however, been extremely difficult for me to forgive myself for some of the things I've done and said in my life. I have hurt people with my actions, my decisions, and my words. I have mentally destroyed people, and much of it has haunted me, and caused me to not live the "Free indeed" life. There are parts of my life where I still need mental liberation. There are conversations that need to be had. There are questions that need to be answered from myself and others.

How would God forgive me if I can't forgive myself? The question I have always had is, "does God really forgive?" There are countless scriptures that tell us He does.

> *"If we confess our sins, He is faithful enough to forgive us." (1 John 1:9)*
>
> *"In him we have redemption through His blood for the forgiveness of sin by His grace." (Ephesians 1:7)*
>
> *"If you forgive those of their trespasses, God will forgive you." (Matthew 6:12)*
>
> *"Forgive, and you will be forgiven." (Matthew 6:14)*
>
> *"Repent, turn, and your sins will be blotted out" (Acts 3:19)*

There are countless others, but as much as I hear these phrases, it is extremely difficult to accept. There are things that I have said and done that have hurt people both physically and mentally. There are things that I've done that still bother me into my adult years. How easy is it for you to know that God has forgiven you for the things you have done? This is still a part of my life that I am working on. It's still a process that is being discovered. This chapter is not complete. I will only know once my soul and His spirit meet after I am no longer here.

If you are reading this book, and I have said, done, or made you feel a certain way, I assure you from the bottom of my heart, I am remorsefully sorry. Please forgive me as I continue to process through trying to forgive myself for actions, and rash decisions I've made in the early stages of my life.

ABOUT THE AUTHOR

Micheal Wellington was born in Baton Rouge, Louisiana. He moved to California with his mother, and siblings in 1988. Micheal attended Granada Hills Kennedy High School, in Granada Hills, California before attending Valencia High School in the Santa Clarita, California. After graduation, he enrolled at California State University, Northridge where he was a member of the track and field team. It was at CSUN that he gained the knowledge and passion for track and field. He graduated in four years and began graduate school to obtain an Elementary California Teacher's Credential.

While in college, he met his wife, Houstina, (Tina) and the two have been together ever since. With the burden of having a family fresh out of college, Micheal was unable to complete the credentialing program and placed it on hold to take care of his family. From there, he began working with children with autism as a behavior therapist, for the next three years. At this point he realized that working with children was supposed to be his purpose.

In January of 2007, Micheal began working at a local high school, Bishop Alemany where he is an educator, history teacher, as well as a track and field head coach. He did have a stint as a varsity, junior varsity, and freshman football coach for 6 years, before placing all of his effort into track and field.

ABOUT THE AUTHOR

Micheal has been told by many administrators, and parents that he has made a huge contribution into the lives of many of the students that have come and gone. Many of them come back after graduation to express the same sentiments.

He became the head coach of the track and field team in 2013. Since then, he has sent 17 kids to college on athletic scholarships. His teams have won a divisional team championship, and finished as runner ups, three times. Thirty-four school records have been broken, have produced seventeen divisional champions, and seven California State medalists.

Micheal is currently a personal trainer, specializing in several arenas, ranging from weight loss, meal plans, speed, agility, hurdles, and overall fitness. The brand name, Your Temple Fitness, was created in 2014 after many of his Facebook followers began asking what they could do for home exercise. He also believes that using and pushing your body with God in mind, is another form of true submission to Him (Romans 12:1).

He has dabbled in modeling, being featured on the book "Brainwashed," by Tom Burrell, been featured on several photography websites, and been a stand-in, in a Nike advertisement.

Michael and Tina, who is a talented fashion designer, have been married since 2003 and live in Southern California, along with their daughter, Grace.

ACKNOWLEDGMENTS

I want to acknowledge all of the people that were a vital part of making the process of this memoir possible. Without you guys, none of the breaking, building, forgiveness of myself and others, or growth would have taken place.

First, to my siblings Catherine, Thomas, and Alveta; I want you guys to know that by being the oldest, I have always been responsible for you. However, I know I could have done a better job, even today. Though it may sound cliché, if you ever need anything, you know what to do.

To Hopes House Ministries, Pastors Charles and Andrea Humphrey; it was in your church where I first learned the difference between religion and a true relationship with Christ. The seed that came from the mission of your church led me to a journey of wholeness.

To Jaumel Farley and Darnell Edwards; it was with you guys and our "startup shops," where I began the process of vulnerability, and learning to hear God's voice.

To Jason Plunkett, Robert Hill, Eric Hunter, Monte Hollomon, and Lawrence Burnett; once our shops became a little larger, it was you guys that prayed for me, pushed me mentally and physically, and encouraged me to go deeper in the Lord; learn to wait on a Him, and continue to wait until He says to move.

It was you that propelled my vulnerability to another level. I HATED it, and still do, but I realize that it is all a part of the process.

To The Waiting Room Church; the intimacy with Christ that we are displaying is doing more than you know. I hope that as this grows, hearing from God will be easier and that more individuals begin to desire the same. To my Grandmother and Uncles: All I can say is thank you a million times. I had so many reasons to not be embraced, but all of you did anyway. Thank you.

ACKNOWLEDGMENTS 109

To my adopted Aunt Charmaine, late uncle, and Manuel White. I thank you for allowing me into your home. It is there where I learned how to work hard, and most importantly, what a family nucleus looked like.

To my brothers from other mothers: Manuel, Chris, Aaron, Marquis Stokes, and Mike; I have known you for pretty much my entire life. I love you because you never held any punches. You always tell it like it is. I would often get offended, but it was all for the good. Only dudes that love you will do that.

To Coach Ernie Gregoire Jr: You did not just fall into the position of being a coach on my staff. You have been more than an assistant coach, and just know that I appreciate you more than you can imagine.

And finally, to my first group of daughters, Alayah, Asia, Asia, Brisa, Chanel, Leah, Nia, Sky, Sojo, Summer, and Summer; I have told you time, and time again, you prepared me well for fatherhood. I experienced every emotion known to man with you girls, but without that experience, Grace would never be able to experience me.

Thank all of you for being a part of this journey. I pray that after you read this book, you too realize that even when you think you weren't, you were always, and will always be loved, regardless of your circumstances and decisions.

www.ingramcontent.com/pod-product-compliance
Lightning Source LLC
Chambersburg PA
CBHW050202130526
44591CB00034B/1945